ABBREVIATIONS

approx	approximately	**patt**	pattern
beg	begin/beginning	**pc**	popcorn
bet	between	**pm**	place marker
BL	back loop(s)	**prev**	previous
BP	back post	**rem**	remain/remaining
BPdc	back post double crochet	**rep**	repeat(s)
CC	contrasting color	**rev sc**	reverse single crochet
ch	chain	**rnd(s)**	round(s)
ch-	refers to chain or space previously made, e.g., ch-1 space	**RS**	right side(s)
		sc	single crochet
ch lp	chain loop	**sc3tog**	single crochet 3 stitches together
ch-sp	chain space	**sk**	skip
CL	cluster(s)	**Sl st**	slip stitch
cm	centimeter(s)	**sp(s)**	space(s)
cont	continue	**st(s)**	stitch(es)
dc	double crochet	**tbl**	through back loop
dc2tog	double crochet 2 stitches together	**tch**	turning chain
dec	decrease/decreases/decreasing	**tog**	together
dtr	double triple crochet	**tr**	triple crochet
FL	front loop(s)	**WS**	wrong side(s)
foll	follow/follows/following	**yd**	yard(s)
FP	front post	**yo**	yarn over
FPdc	front post double crochet	**yoh**	yarn over hook
FPtr	front post triple crochet	**[ ]**	Work instructions within brackets as many times as directed
g	gram(s)		
hdc	half double crochet	**( )**	At end of row, indicates total number of stitches worked
inc	increase/increases/increasing		
lp(s)	loop(s)	*****	Repeat instructions following the single asterisk as directed
m	meter(s)		
MC	main color	******	Repeat instructions between asterisks as many times as directed or repeat from a given set of instructions
mm	millimeter(s)		
oz	ounce(s)		
p	picot		

Baby Diamonds
BLANKET

This entrelac baby blanket is worked in adjoining strips of squares turned on their points. The pattern is a little challenging at first, but once mastered, it is quite easy. The blanket is worked in Tunisian crochet, but you can use a regular hook because there are never more than seven stitches on the hook at a time.

YARN
Medium-weight acrylic yarn in 3 colors
Green: 800 yd (740 m)
Yellow: 400 yd (370 m)
White: 400 yd (370 m)

HOOK
9/I (5.5 mm)

STITCHES USED
Tunisian
Single crochet
Double crochet

GAUGE
1 square = 1½" (3.8 cm)

NOTION
Tapestry needle

FINISHED SIZE
34" ✕ 42" (86.5 ✕ 107 cm)

Interlocking squares of Tunisian crochet are turned on their points.

BLANKET

Entrelac patt is worked entirely from RS. When 1 strip is completed, fasten off that yarn, join new yarn at beg of row, and start again. To even out ends, every other color strip begins and ends with a half square (triangle). Each square or triangle in strip consists of 5 rows. Refer to page 9 for detailed instructions for Tunisian st.

STRIP 1
Begins and ends with triangle.

With MC, ch 144 loosely.

Beg Triangle, Row 1: Draw up lp in second ch from hook (2 lps on hook), yo, draw through both lps.

Row 2: Insert hook bet first 2 vertical bars and pick up lp (inc made), pick up lp in next ch (3 lps on hook), [yo, draw through 2 lps] 2 times (1 lp left on hook).

*Row 3: Insert hook bet first 2 bars and pick up lp (inc made), draw up lp from under next bar and next ch (4 lps on hook), [yo, draw through 2 lps] 3 times (1 lp left on hook).

Cont in this manner, having 1 st more each row, until you have 7 lps on hook (row 5), work off as before.

Bind off: Insert hook under next bar, draw yarn through bar and lp on hook (Sl st worked). Cont to work Sl st through each bar to end.* Sl st in same ch as last lp of row 5. Do not fasten off, but cont to first square.

Square 1, Row 1 (still on first color strip): Draw up lp in each of next 6 ch (7 lps on hook), [yo, draw through 2 lps] 6 times (1 lp left on hook). This lp is the first lp of the foll row.

Row 2: Insert hook under next bar, draw yarn through (2 lps on hook), draw up lp in each of next 4 bars, draw up lp in next ch (7 lps on hook), work off lps as for row 1 of square.

Rows 3–5: Rep row 2.

Bind off: Sl st in each bar to end, Sl st in same ch as last lp of row 5.

Squares 2–13: Work same as square 1 (6 ch left at end of row).

End Triangle, Row 1 (end of first color strip): Draw up lp in each of 6 rem ch (7 lps on hook), work off as before.

Row 2: Draw up 5 lps (6 lps on hook), work off as before.

Cont in this manner, always having 1 less lp each row, until 1 lp rem, fasten off. This completes first color strip.

STRIP 2
Begins and ends with a square. Each square has 5 rows.

Square 1, Row 1: With A, pick up 1 lp in each of 6 Sl sts of beg triangle, pick up lp in end of first row of first square on strip 1 (7 lps on hook), work off lps.

Complete square as for rows 2–5 of square 1 of first strip.

Bind off: Sl st in each bar to end, having last Sl st in last row (top point) of same square.

Squares 2–14: Work same as square 1, picking up first row of sts in slipped sts, then under bars in subsequent rows. End strip with completed square.

STRIP 3
Begins and ends with a triangle.

Beg Triangle: With MC, ch 2, draw up lp in first ch from hook and pick up lp in side of first row of first square of strip 2 (3 lps on hook), [yo, draw through 2 lps] 2 times. Rep from * to * of beg triangle, strip 1. Sl st in first bound off st of square 1, strip 2.

Work squares of strip same as squares of strip 2. End with triangle, same as end triangle, strip 1.

Peaks of the border echo the blanket's diamond motif.

REMAINING STRIPS

Work same as strips 2 and 3 in this color sequence: B, MC, A, MC, ending with MC (39 strips).

CLOSING TRIANGLES

Worked across top and bottom to even off edges.

Row 1: With MC, at top right corner, pick up 6 lps along bound off edge of first square, plus 1 lp in end of first row of second square (7 lps on hook), work off as before.

Row 2: Sk first bar, pick up 5 lps so you only have 6 lps on hook, work off as before.

Row 3: Sk first bar, pick up 4 lps (5 lps on hook), work off as before.

Row 4: Sk first bar, pick up 3 lps (4 lps on hook), work off as before.

Row 5: Sk first bar, pick up 2 lps (3 lps on hook), work off as before, 1 lp on hook, Sl st into last side st (at top).

Cont across top edge in this manner. Work same closing triangles across bottom edge.

BORDER

Row 1: Using MC, starting in top right corner, RS facing you, ch 1, work 1 sc in same st (half corner), * work sc along short edge, picking up 96 sts along this end, 3 sc in corner, sc along long end, picking up 126 sts along this end,

3 sc in corner, rep from * once, ending with 1 sc in same st as beg, join with Sl st to beg ch 1 (this forms last corner).

Row 2: Ch 3, work 2 dc in same st (half corner), * sk 2 sts, 1 sc in next st, sk 2 sts, [3 dc, ch 2, 3 dc] in next st, rep from * all around, ending with 3 dc in same st as beg ch 3, ch 2, join with Sl st to form last corner, fasten off.

FINISHING
Weave in ends using tapestry needle.

BASIC TUNSIAN STITCH
Each row has 2 halves: picking up the loops and working them off.

Make a chain of the desired length.

Row 1 (first half): Keeping all loops on the hook, skip the first chain from the hook (the loop on the hook is the first chain) and draw up a loop in each chain across **(1)**. Do not turn.

Row 1 (second half): Wrap the yarn over the hook and draw it through the first loop * Wrap the yarn over the hook and draw it through the next 2 loops. Repeat from * across until 1 loop remains. The loop that remains on the hook always counts as the first stitch of the next row **(2)**.

Row 2 (first half): Keeping all loops on the hook, skip the first vertical bar and draw up a loop under the next vertical bar and under each vertical bar across **(3)**.

Row 2 (second half): Work the same as the second half of row 1.

Repeat row 2 for basic Tunisian stitch.

Heirloom Baby
BLANKET

Dainty shell stitches are traditional for baby blankets. Using this easy pattern, you can crochet a special blanket that will become a family keepsake. The blanket is made in one piece, with rows of shells divided by ridges formed of front post and back post double crochet stitches.

Front post and back post double crochet stitches form ridges between shells.

HEIRLOOM BABY BLANKET

YARN
Medium-weight acrylic yarn
1,400 yd (1,200 m)

HOOK
8/H (5 mm)

STITCHES USED
Double crochet
Front post double crochet
Back post double crochet

GAUGE
3 shell patterns = 4" (10 cm)

NOTION
Tapestry needle

FINISHED SIZE
30" × 40" (76 × 102 cm)

BLANKET
Blanket is worked in 1 piece.

Foundation row: Ch 121. Starting in fifth ch from hook, * work [2 dc, ch 2, 2 dc] in same st (shell made), sk 2 ch, 1 dc in next ch, sk 2 ch, rep from * across, end sk 2 ch, 1 dc in last ch (20 shells), turn.

Row 1: Ch 3, * work [2 dc, ch 2, 2 dc] in next ch-2 sp, 1 FPdc over next dc, rep from * across, end 1 dc in top of tch, turn.

Row 2: Ch 3, * work [2 dc, ch 2, 2 dc] in next ch-2 sp, 1 BPdc over next dc, rep from * across, end 1 dc in top of tch, turn.

Rep rows 1 and 2 for 40" (102 cm), fasten off.

FINISHING
Weave in ends using tapestry needle.

Baby-Soft
BLANKET

Some yarns today are made with fibers so soft, you just can't stop touching them. Imagine what a pleasure it is to crochet with them, feeling baby-soft texture running through your fingers. This blanket is sure to comfort any baby.

BLANKET

Blanket is worked in 1 piece.

Foundation row: Using A, ch 63 loosely. Beg in third ch from hook, work [1 sc, 1 dc] in same ch, * sk 1 ch, [1 sc, 1 dc] in next ch, rep from * across, end 1 dc in last ch, turn.

Row 1: Ch 2, sk first st and first dc, work [1 sc, 1 dc] in next sc, * sk next dc, [1 sc, 1 dc] in next sc, rep from * across, end 1 dc in top of tch, turn.

Rep row 1, working 10 rows in A, 2 rows in B. (It is okay to carry A loosely up 2 rows of B, but you will have to cut B and restart each time.) Cont in this manner until you have 6 A stripes and 5 B stripes, do not fasten off, turn.

BORDER

Row 1: With right side facing you, cont with A, * work 1 sc in each sc across to corner (62 sts), 3 sc in corner, cont along side, 10 sc in each A section, 2 sc in each B section (70 sc), 3 sc in corner, rep from * once, ending with 3 sc in last corner, join with Sl st to first sc.

Row 2: With A, ch 2, * work 1 hdc in each st to center of next corner, 3 hdc in center of corner, rep from * 3 times more, ending with Sl st to top of beg ch 2, pick up lp with B, fasten off A.

Row 3: With B, rep row 2.

Row 4: With B, * work 1 sc in next st, ch 3, rep from * all around, fasten off.

FINISHING

Weave in ends using tapestry needle.

YARN

Bulky-weight acrylic bouclé and nylon eyelash blend yarn in 2 colors
Blue: 575 yd (529 m)
White: 246 yd (226 m)

HOOK

11/L (8 mm)

STITCHES USED

Single crochet
Double crochet
Half double crochet

GAUGE

$4\frac{1}{2}$ clusters = 4" (10 cm) (cluster = 1 sc, 1 dc in same st)

NOTION

Tapestry needle

FINISHED SIZE

36" X 40" (91.5 X 102 cm)

Rainbow Blocks
BLANKET

This colorful blanket is a great gift for a toddler or preschooler. Because it will get lots of use, the blanket is crocheted from yarn that can be machine laundered. The rainbow blocks are actually crocheted in strips that can be sewn together quickly.

Machine washable yarn in tiny shell pattern of single crochet and chain stitches.

YARN
Medium-weight smooth yarn in 6 colors
Blue: 400 yd (368 m)
Yellow: 200 yd (184 m)
Orange: 200 yd (184 m)
Rose: 200 yd (184 m)
Red: 200 yd (184 m)
Green: 200 yd (184 m)

HOOK
10/J (6 mm)

STITCHES USED
Single crochet
Half double crochet
Double crochet

GAUGE
5 small shells = 4" (10 cm)

NOTION
Tapestry needle

FINISHED SIZE
36" × 36" (91.5 × 91.5 cm)

BLANKET

Color sequence of squares in each strip (left to right):

Strip 1: red, green, rose, yellow, orange, blue, red
Strip 2: green, rose, yellow, orange, blue, red, blue
Strip 3: rose, yellow, orange, blue, red, blue, orange
Strip 4: yellow, orange, blue, red, blue, orange, yellow
Strip 5: orange, blue, red, blue, orange, yellow, rose
Strip 6: blue, red, blue, orange, yellow, rose, green
Strip 7: red, blue, orange, yellow, rose, green, red

Foll the above color sequence, make 7 strips as foll:

Foundation row: Ch 22. Starting in third ch from hook, *work [1 sc, ch 2, 1 sc] all in same ch (small shell made), sk 1, rep from * across, end 1 hdc in last ch, turn (9 small shells).

Row 1: Ch 2 (counts as a hdc), * work [1 sc, ch 2, 1 sc] all in ch-2 sp of next small shell, rep from * 6 times more, end 1 hdc in top of tch, turn.

Rep row 1 for 5" (12.7 cm). Pull up new color on last row, and cont next color in sequence. Cont in this manner until all 7 color blocks are made. Fasten off.

FINISHING

Sew all strips tog using tapestry needle. Weave in ends.

BORDER

Row 1: With blue, RS facing you, join yarn in any corner. Working in sc, work 1 sc in corner (half corner), * 14 sc in each color block, [1 sc, ch 1, 1 sc] in corner, rep from * 3 times more, ending with 1 sc in last st, ch 1, join with Sl st to first sc (completing corner).

Row 2: Ch 3 (half corner), * [sk 1 sc, work 1 dc in next sc, 1 dc in skipped sc] 49 times, [1 dc, ch 2, 1 dc] in ch-1 sp of corner, rep from * 3 times more, ending with 1 dc in last st, ch 2, join with Sl st in last corner sp.

Baby SWEATER and HAT

This adorable baby sweater and hat set combines the technique of working a garment from the top down and using granny squares. Lightweight cotton yarn makes it comfortable for baby and easy to care for.

Made with 3 colors: MC, A, and B.

V-stitch (V-st): (1 dc, ch 1, 1 dc) in same st or sp.

Beginning cluster (beg cluster): Ch 3, [yo, insert hook in st or sp, yo, draw up a loop, yo, draw through 2 lps] twice in same st or sp, yo, draw through 3 loops on hook.

Cluster: [Yo, insert hook in st or sp, yo, draw up a loop, yo, draw through 2 loops on hook] 3 times in same st or sp, yo, draw through 4 loops on hook.

Single crochet 2 together (sc2tog): [Insert hook in next st, yo, draw yarn through st] twice, yo, draw yarn through 3 loops on hook.

Picot: Ch 3, sc in 3rd ch from hook.

Each V-st inc adds 2 sts. Sweater yoke is worked from the neck down.

SWEATER

Starting at neck edge, with MC, ch 58 (64).

Row 1: 1 dc in 4th ch from hook (counts as 2 dc), 1 dc in each of next 7 (8) ch (right front section), V-st in next ch (inc made), 1 dc in each of next 9 (10) ch (right sleeve section), V-st in next ch, 1 dc in each of the next 16 (18) ch (back section), V-st in next ch, 1 dc in each of next 9 (10) ch (left sleeve section), V-st in next ch, 1 dc in each of last 9 (10) ch (left front section), turn. There will be 9 (10) dc in each front section; 9 (10) dc in each sleeve section; 16 (18) dc in back section; sections will be divided by a V-st.

Row 2: Ch 3 (counts as a dc, now and throughout), sk first dc, *1 dc in each dc to next V-st, V-st in ch-1 sp of next V-st, rep from * 3 times, 1 dc in each dc to end, 1 dc in top of turning ch, turn.

Rows 3–13 (3–14): Rep row 3, inc 8 sts in every row. There will be 22 (24) sts on right front, 35 (38) on sleeve, 42 (46) sts on back, 35 (38) on sleeve, 22 (24) sts on left front: 156 (170) dc plus 4 ch-1 sps total.

DIVIDE FOR SLEEVES AND BODY

Row 1: Ch 3, sk first dc, dc on each of next 21 (23) sts of left front, ch 2, sk next 35 (38) dc of left sleeve, dc in each of next 42 (46) dc of back, ch 2, sk next 35 (38) dc of right sleeve, dc in each of last 21 (23) dc of right front, 1 dc in top of turning ch, turn (86 [94] dc).

Row 2: Ch 3, sk first dc, 1 dc in each of next 21 (23) sts, 1 dc in each of next 2 ch sts at underarm, 1 dc in each of the next 42 (48) dc, 1 dc in each of next 2 ch sts at underarm, 1 dc in each of the last 21 (23) dc, 1 dc in top of turning ch, turn (90 [98] dc). Fasten off.

LIGHTWEIGHT COTTON YARN IN THREE COLORS
MC: 438 yd (403 m)
A and B: 146 yd (135 m) (will make both sweater and hat)

HOOKS
Sweater: F/5 (3.75 mm) for size 2 and 4 yoke
F/5 (3.75 mm) for size 2 squares
G/6 (4 mm) for size 4 squares
Hat: F/5 (3.75 mm) for size 2; G/6 (4 mm) for size 4

GAUGE
1 square = 5" x 5" (12.5 x 12.5 cm) with F/5
(3.75 mm) hook
1 square = 5½" x 5½" (14 x 14 cm) with G/6 (4 mm) hook
18 dc = 4" (10 cm) with F/5 (3.75 mm) hook

NOTIONS
Tapestry needle

FINISHED SIZE
Sweater: sizes 2 (4)
Finished chest: 22" (24)" (56 [61] cm)
Hat: 16" (40.5 cm) in circumference; 6" (15 cm) deep for size 2
17½" (44.5 cm) in circumference, 7½" (19 cm) deep for size 4

SKILL LEVEL
Intermediate

SQUARES

Make 4 Kaleidoscope Squares as follows:

Foundation: With A, ch 6, join with a Sl st to form a ring.

Rnd 1: With A, ch 4 (counts as dc, ch 1), [1 dc, ch 1] 7 times in ring, join with a Sl st in 3rd ch of beg ch-3 (8 ch-1 sp).

Rnd 2: With A, ch 3 (counts as dc), 1 dc in next ch-1 sp, *ch 2, 2 dc in next ch-1 sp, rep from * 6 times, ch 2, join with a Sl st in the 3rd ch of beg ch-3 (8 groups of 2 dc, 8 ch-1 sps). Fasten off A.

Rnd 3: With right side facing, join B in any ch-2 sp, ch 3, (beg cluster, ch 2, cluster, ch 2) in first sp, (cluster, ch 2, cluster, ch 2) in each ch-2 sp around, join with a Sl st in 3rd ch of beg ch-3 (8 clusters, 16 ch-2 sps). Drop B to wrong side.

Rnd 4: With right side facing, join MC in first ch-2 sp, ch 3, (beg cluster, ch 2, cluster) in first sp, ch 3 sk next ch-2 sp, *[1 cluster, ch 3] 3 times in next ch-2 sp, sk next ch-2 sp**, [cluster, ch 3] twice in next ch-2 sp, sk next ch-2 sp, rep from * twice, rep from * to ** once, join with a Sl st in 3rd ch of beg ch-3 (4 groups of 3 clusters, 4 groups of 2 clusters). Drop MC to wrong side.

Rnd 5: With right side facing, join A in first ch-3 sp be-tween any 2-cluster group, ch 3, 2 dc in same sp (half corner made), *ch 2, 2 dc in next ch-3 sp, (ch 1, 1 sc) in each of next 2 ch-3 sp, ch 1, 2 dc in next ch-3 sp, ch 2**, (3 dc, ch 3, 3 dc) in next ch-3 sp (corner), rep from * twice, rep from * to ** once, 3 dc in same sp as first half corner, ch 3, join with a Sl st in 3rd ch of beg ch-3. Drop A to wrong side, pick up B.

Rnd 6: With B, ch 1, starting in same st, *1 sc in each of next 3 dc, 2 sc in next ch-2 sp, 1 sc in each of next 2 dc, [1 sc in next ch-1 sp, 1 sc in next sc] twice, 1 sc in next ch-1 sp, 1 sc in each of next 2 dc, 2 sc in next ch-2 sp, 1 sc in each of next 3 dc, (1 sc, ch 3, 1 sc) in next ch-3 sp (corner made), rep from * around, join with a Sl st in first sc.

Rnd 7: With B, ch 1, 1 sc in each sc across to next corner, (1 sc, ch 3, 1 sc) in next ch-3 sp, rep from * 3 times, 1 sc in next sc, join with a Sl st in first sc (21 sc between each corner ch-3 sp). Fasten off B. Pick up MC and draw through loop on hook.

Rnd 8: With MC, ch 1, 1 sc in each sc across to next cor-ner, (1 sc, ch 3, 1 sc) in next ch-3 sp, rep from * 3 times, 1 sc in each of next 2 sc, join with a Sl st in first sc (23 sc between each corner ch-3 sp). Fasten off MC.

With MC, sew 4 squares together in a strip, sew squares to bottom edge of yoke fronts and back. This will also join sleeve tops at underarms.

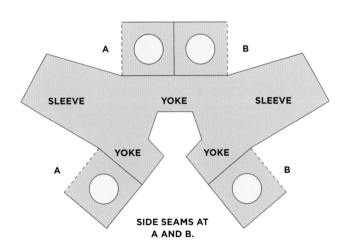

SLEEVE (MAKE 2)

Sleeves are worked back and forth in rows, using the F/5 (3.75 mm) hook for both sizes.

With right side facing, join MC at underarm in 2nd added ch at underarm.

Row 1: Ch 3, 1 dc in each of the next 35 (38) dc, 1 dc in the rem ch at underarm, turn 37 (40) dc.

Row 2: Ch 3, 1 dc in each dc around, turn.

Rep row 2 until sleeve measures 5" (5½") (12.5 [14] cm) from beg. Drop MC to wrong side.

Sleeve border:

Row 1: With right side facing, join B in first dc, ch 1, starting in same st, 1 sc in each st across, turn.

Rows 2-8: Rep row 1 working in the following color sequence: 1 more row B, 2 rows MC, 1 row A, 1 row B, 1 row MC.

Row 9: With MC, *ch 3, sk next sc, 1 sc in next sc, rep from * across. Fasten off, leaving a long sewing length for sewing underarm seam.

Edging:

Edging is worked around entire outer edges of garment.

With F/5 (3.75 mm) hook for size 2, G/6 (4 mm) hook for size 4:

Rnd 1: With right side facing, join MC at underarm seam of bottom right side, ch 1, 1 sc in each sc along bottom of square, 3 sc in corner, 1 sc in each sc along front edge of square, sc evenly spd across row–end sts of yoke to top of right front, 3 sc in corner, sc in each st across neck edge to top of left front, 3 sc in corner, 1 sc evenly spd across row–end sts of yoke to beg of square, 1 sc in each sc along front edge of square, 3 sc in corner, 1 sc in each sc along bottom edge, join with a Sl st in first sc. Drop MC to wrong side, join B.

Rnd 2: With B, ch 1, sc in each sc around, working 3 sc in each corner sc, join with a Sl st in first sc.

Rnds 3-5: Rep rnd 2 working in the following color sequence: 1 rnd each of A, B, and MC.

Rnd 6: With MC, ch 1, sc in first sc, picot, sk next st, *1 sc in next sc, picot, sk next st, rep from * around, join with a Sl st in first sc. Fasten off.

Tie: With G/6 (hook, and all 3 colors held together as one, ch 100. Fasten off.

Weave the tie in and out of the picot row at the neck, leaving ends to form a bow.

Blocking: Place garment on a padded surface, sprinkle lightly with water, pat into shape, using rust proof pins, pin to hold shape, allow to dry.

HAT

Make 3 Kaleidoscope Squares (opposite) in same color sequence as sweater. Join squares together to form a tube, using the chain join method joining with wrong sides together so that ch is on right side of squares.

Crown:

Rnd 1: With right side facing, join MC in any seam (mark this st as beg of round), ch 1,sk first, 1 sc in each sc along top of square, 2 sc in each joining seam, join with Sl st in first sc (80 sc).

Rnd 2: Ch 1, starting in same st, *1 sc in each of the next 8 sc, sc2tog over next 2 sts, rep from * around, join with Sl st in first sc (72 sc).

Rnd 3: Ch 1, starting in same st, *1 sc in each of the next 8 sc, sc2tog over next 2 sts, rep from * around, join with Sl st in first sc (64 sc).

Rnds 4-9: Continue in this manner, dec 8 sc each rnd, always having 1 st less sc between dec, until 16 sc rem. Fasten off, leaving a 12" (30.5 cm) sewing length. With tapestry needle and sewing length, weave needle through last rnd of sts, gather tight, sew top together several times to secure. Fasten off.

Bottom Border:

Rnd 1: With right side facing, join MC in any seam on bottom edge of hat, ch 1, 1 sc in each sc along bottom of square, 2 sc in each joining seam, join with a Sl st in first sc (81 sc).

Rnd 2: Ch 1, 1 sc in first sc, ch 3, (sc, ch 3) in each sc round, join with a Sl st in first sc. Fasten off.

Cozy Baby HAT

A baby hat is such a perfect newborn gift that I couldn't resist including just one. This is a super-soft hat with earflaps and a twist on top.

YARN
Lightweight alpaca yarn in two colors
125 yd (115 m) each

HOOKS
5/F (3.75 mm)
6/G (4 mm)

STITCHES USED
Single crochet
Single crochet through back loop
Double crochet
Reverse single crochet

GAUGE
9 clusters = 4" (10 cm) using 6/G hook
6 rows of band = 1" (2.5 cm) using 5/F hook

NOTION
Tapestry needle

FINISHED SIZE
14" (35.5 cm)
head circumference

HAT

Begin with bottom band as follows:

Foundation row: Using 5/F hook and A, ch 11. Starting in second ch from hook, work 1 sc in each ch to end (10 sc), ch 1 (counts as sc now and throughout), turn.

Row 1: Working tbl, sk first st, work 1 sc in each st across.

Rep row 1 for 84 rows, do not fasten off.

Still using A, pick up 72 sc, evenly spaced, along row ends (long side of band). This will be RS of your work. Ch 1, turn.

Change to 6/G hook and work patt as foll:

Foundation row: Sk first st, work 1 sc in next st, * 1 sc, 1 dc in next st, sk 1, rep from * across, ending 1 sc in tch, ch 2, turn.

Row 1: * Work [1 sc, 1 dc] in next st, rep from * 33 times, end1 dc in tch (34 CL), ch 1, turn.

Row 2: Work 1 dc in same st as tch, * [1 sc, 1 dc] in next st, rep from * 34 times, end 1 sc in tch (35 CL), do not fasten off A, join B.

Rep rows 1 and 2, alternating A and B every two rows for 12 more rows, ch 1, turn. Fasten off B and complete top shaping with A as foll:

Row 1: * Sc in each of next 8 sts, sc2tog, rep from * across, end 1 sc (65 sts), ch 1, turn.

Row 2: Sk first st, sc in each of next 2 sts, sc2tog, * sc in each of next 5 sts, sc2tog, rep from * across, end 5 sc (56 sts), ch 1, turn.

Row 3: Sk first st, sc2tog, * sc in each of next 3 sts, sc2tog, rep from * across (45 sts), ch 1, turn.

Row 4: Sk first st, sc2tog, * sc in each of next 3 sts, sc2tog, rep from * across (36 sts), ch 1, turn.

Row 5: Sk first st, sc2tog, * sc in each of next 3 sts, sc2tog, rep from * across (29 sts), ch 1, turn.

Row 6: Sk first st, sc2tog, * sc in each of next 3 stitches, sc2tog, rep from * across, end 1 sc (23 sts), ch 1, turn.

Row 7: Sk first st, sc2tog across (12 sts), ch 1, turn.

Row 8: Sc2tog across row, fasten off, leaving long end for sewing.

Shell-stitch rows in alternating colors form the crown.

Single crochet stitches worked through the back loop create a "ribbed" bottom band.

EARFLAPS

Make two.

Foundation row: With A, ch 13. Starting in second ch from hook, work 1 sc in each ch (12 sc), ch 1, turn.

Row 1: Sk first st, work 1 sc in each st across, ch 1, turn.

Rows 2, 3, and 4: Rep row 1.

Row 5: Sk first st, sc2tog, sc to last 3 sts, sc2tog, sc in last st, ch 1, turn.

Row 6: Rep row 1.

Cont to rep rows 5 and 1 until 4 sts rem, sc2tog twice, turn, sc2tog, fasten off, leaving long end for sewing.

TOP TWISTS

Make four.

Using double strand of any leftover yarn, ch 25, turn, work 2 sc in each ch, fasten off, leaving a long end to attach to top of hat.

FINISHING

1. Sew the back seam of the hat, using a tapestry needle and the long yarn that was left, weave in end.

2. Fold the bottom band in half to the inside, and sew in place, weave in end.

3. With B and 5/F hook, work 1 row sc into bottom fold of band, do not turn. Work 1 row rev sc around bottom of hat, fasten off, weave in end.

4. Sew the earflaps in place under the reverse crochet row using long yarn that was left, leaving 1" (2.5 cm) space on each side of the back seam. Weave in ends.

5. With B and 5/F hook, starting at top corner of one earflap, RS facing you, pick up 14 sc down to point, ch 45 for tie, work sc up the ch sts, then cont on other side of earflap, fasten off, weave in ends. Rep for the other earflap.

6. Sew twists to top of hat.

Blackberry Stitch
SWEATER *and* HAT

BLACKBERRY STITCH
SWEATER AND HAT

BACK

Notes:

1. Blackberry stitch (bbs): Draw up a lp in the next sc (yo, draw through last loop on hook) 3 times, forming a chain, keeping the ch 3 just made to front of work, yo, and draw through both loops on hook (blackberry stitch completed).

2. Sc2tog: Insert hook in next st, yo, draw yarn through st, insert hook in next st, yo, draw yarn through st, yo, draw yarn through 3 lps on hook.

With larger hook, ch 52 (56, 60).

Foundation row: Starting in 2nd ch from hook, 1 sc in each ch across, turn—51 (55, 59) sc.

Row 1 (RS): Ch 1 (counts as first sc), sk first sc, *work a blackberry stitch (bbs) in next sc, 1 sc in next sc; rep from * across, ending with 1 sc in top of tch, turn—51 (55, 59) sts.

Row 2: Ch 1 (counts as first sc), sk first st, 1 sc in each st across, 1 sc in top of tch, turn—51 (55, 59) sts.

Row 3: Ch 1 (counts as first sc), sk first sc, 1 sc next sc, *bbs in next sc, sc in next sc, rep from * across, ending with 1 sc in top of tch—51 (55, 59) sts.

Row 4: Rep Row 2.

Rep Rows 1–4 for pattern.

Work even in patt until Back measures 6½ (7, 7½)" [16.5 (18, 19) cm] from beg, ending with a WS row.

Shape Armhole

Sl st to 3rd st, work in established patt across to within last 2 sts, turn, leaving remaining sts unworked.

Work even in established patt on center 47 (51, 55) sts until armhole measures 5 (5½, 6)" [12.5 (14, 15) cm] from beg. End off.

YARN
Lightweight smooth yarn 720 yd (663 m)

HOOKS
Size E-4 (3.5 mm)
Size F-5 (3.75 mm) or size to obtain correct gauge

STITCHES
Chain stitch
Single crochet
Blackberry stitch

GAUGE
18 sts = 4" (10 cm) in pattern stitch with larger hook
Take time to check gauge.

NOTIONS/SUPPLIES
Tapestry needle
Three ½" (1.3 cm) buttons
Sewing needle and thread

SIZE
12 mo (18 mo, 24 mo)
Finished chest: 22 (24, 26)" [56 (61, 66) cm]
Hat circumference: 16 (17, 18)" [40.5 (43, 45.5) cm]

LEFT FRONT

With larger hook, ch 28 (30, 32).

Foundation row: Starting in 2nd ch from hook, 1 sc in each ch across, turn—27 (29, 31) sc.

Work in bbs patt same as Back on 27 (29, 31) sts, rep Rows 1–4 for patt until piece measures 6½ (7, 7½)" [16.5 (18, 19) cm] from beg, ending with a WS row.

Shape Armhole

Sl st to 3rd st, work in established patt across, turn.

Work even in established patt on 25 (27, 29) sts until armhole measures 3 (3½, 4)" [7.5 (9, 10) cm] from beg, ending with an RS row at neck edge.

Shape Neck

Sl st over first 11 (12, 13) sts, ch 1, sk next st, work in established patt across rem 14 (15, 16) sts, turn.

Cont working in established patt, dec 1 st at neck edge on each of next 3 rows. Work even on rem 11 (12, 13) sts until armhole measures 5 (5½, 6)" [12.5 (14. 15) cm] from beg. End off.

RIGHT FRONT

Work same as Left Front to armhole, ending with a WS row.

Shape Armhole

Work in established patt across first 25 (27, 29) sts, turn, leaving rem 2 sts unworked. Work even in established patt on 25 (27, 29) sts until armhole measures 3 (3½, 4)" [7.5 (9, 10) cm] from beg, ending with an RS row at armhole edge.

Shape Neck

Work in established patt across first 14 (15, 16) sts, turn, leaving rem 11 (12, 13) sts unworked.

Cont working in established patt, dec 1 st at neck edge on each of next 3 rows. Work even on rem 11 (12, 13) sts until armhole measures 5 (5½, 6)" [12.5 (14. 15) cm] from beg. End off.

SLEEVES

Cuff: With smaller hook, ch 34 (36, 38).

Foundation Row: Starting in 2nd ch from hook, 1 sc in each ch across, turn—33 (35, 37) sc.

Row 1: Ch 1 (counts as first sc), sk first st, working BL of sts, 1 sc in each sc across, 1 sc in top of tch, turn—33 (35, 37) sts.

Rows 2–4: Rep Row 1.

Row 5: Ch 1 (counts as first sc), working in sc in both loops of sts, increase 14 sts evenly spaced across, turn—47 (49, 51) sts.

With smaller hook, work even in bbs patt same as Back until Sleeve measures 1" (2.5 cm) from top of Cuff. Change to larger hook, and cont working in established patt until Sleeve measures 7 (7½, 8)" [18 (19, 20.5) cm] from beg. End off.

Finishing

With RS of pieces facing each other, pin shoulder seams, then sew shoulder seams. Fold Sleeves in half lengthwise, with center top of Sleeve at shoulder seam, pin then sew Sleeves into armhole. Sew underarm and side seams.

Neckband

Note: Neckband starts and finishes ½" (1.3 cm) in from edges to allow for overlap when buttoned.

Row 1: With smaller hook and RS facing, and starting ½" (1.3 cm) to the left of Right Front edge, join yarn in next st on neck edge, ch 1 (counts as first sc), work 17 (18, 19) sc evenly spaced across Right Front neck shaping to shoulder seam, work 30 (32, 34) sc across Back neck edge, work 18 (19, 20) sc evenly spaced across Left Front neck shaping, stopping ½" (1.3 cm) from Left Front edge, turn—66 (70, 74) sts.

Rows 2–5: Ch 1 (counts as first sc), sk first st, working in BL of sts, sc in each st across, sc in top of tch, turn. End off.

Starting just below neck edge on Left Front, sew buttons ¾" (2 cm) apart down left front edge. No need to make buttonholes, use open spaces bet sts as buttonholes.

Blocking is not recommended for textured stitches. If some blocking is required, spritz lightly with water, pat gently into place with fingers, allow to dry flat.

HAT

With smaller hook, ch 74 (78, 82).

Foundation row: Starting in 2nd ch from hook, 1 sc in each ch across, turn—73 (77, 81) sc.

Work in bbs patt same as Back on 73 (77, 81) sts, rep Rows 1–4 for patt until piece measures 6 (6½, 7)" [15 (16.5, 18) cm] from beg, ending with a WS row.

Shape crown as follows:

Row 1: Ch 1 (counts as first sc), sk first st, 1 sc in each st across, 1 sc in top of tch, turn—73 (77, 81) sts.

Row 2: Ch 1 (counts as first sc), sk first st, working in sc in BL of sts, dec 3 (7, 11) sts evenly spaced across, turn—70 sts.

Row 3: Ch 1 (counts as first sc), sk first st, working in sc in BL of sts, sc in each of next 4 sts, sc2tog in next 2 sts, *1 sc in each of the next 5 sc, sc2tog in next 2 sts; rep from * across, turn—60 sts.

Row 4: Ch 1 (counts as first sc), sk first st, working in sc in BL of sts, sc in each of next 3 sts, sc2tog in next 2 sts, *1 sc in each of the next 4 sc, sc2tog in next 2 sts; rep from * across, turn—50 sts.

Row 5: Ch 1 (counts as first sc), sk first st, working in sc in BL of sts, sc in each of next 2 sts, sc2tog in next 2 sts, *1 sc in each of the next 3 sc, sc2tog in next 2 sts; rep from * across, turn—40 sts.

Row 6: Ch 1 (counts as first sc), sk first st, working in sc in BL of sts, sc in next st, sc2tog in next 2 sts, *1 sc in each of the next 2 sc, sc2tog in next 2 sts; rep from * across, turn—30 sts.

Row 7: Ch 1 (counts as first sc), sk first st, sc2tog in next 2 sts, *1 sc in next st, sc2tog in next 2 sts; rep from * across, turn—20 sts.

Row 8: Ch 1 (counts as first sc), sk first st, *sc2tog in next 2 sts; rep from * across, ending with 1 sc in top of tch, turn—11 sts. End off, leaving an 18" (45.5 cm) sewing length. Thread this end on a tapestry needle, gather sts along last row and draw up. Draw through again and knot, then sew back seam.

Corkscrews

Make 3.

With larger hook, using yarn double-stranded, ch 21. Starting in 2nd ch from hook, work 3 sc in each ch across. End off, leaving sewing length. Sew to top of hat.

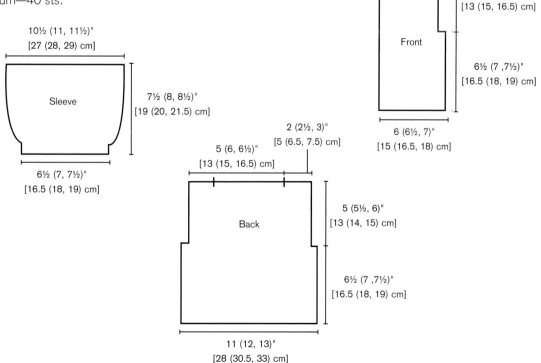

10½ (11, 11½)"
[27 (28, 29) cm]

Sleeve

7½ (8, 8½)"
[19 (20, 21.5) cm]

6½ (7, 7½)"
[16.5 (18, 19) cm]

2 (2½, 3)"
[5 (6.5, 7.5) cm]

5 (6, 6½)"
[13 (15, 16.5) cm]

Back

5 (5½, 6)"
[13 (14, 15) cm]

6½ (7, 7½)"
[16.5 (18, 19) cm]

11 (12, 13)"
[28 (30.5, 33) cm]

5 (6, 6½)"
[13 (15, 16.5) cm]

Front

6½ (7, 7½)"
[16.5 (18, 19) cm]

6 (6½, 7)"
[15 (16.5, 18) cm]

Eight-Pocket CARRYALL

You can never have too many closets or too many pockets. Get organized with this great big tote with places for all your baby's essentials. Interesting texture is created by alternating single and double crochet stitches in one row, then working singles in the doubles and doubles in the singles in the next row.

EIGHT-POCKET
CARRYALL

YARN
Medium weight cotton yarn
MC: 944 yd (868 m)
CC: 236 yd (217 m)

HOOKS
9/I (5.5 mm)
8/H (5 mm)

STITCHES USED
Single crochet
Double crochet

GAUGE
13 sts = 4" (10 cm) on 9/I hook

NOTIONS
Tapestry needle
Button

FINISHED SIZE
16" x 12" x 3"
(40.5 x 30.5 x 7.5 cm)

Cotton yarn in alternating single and double crochet stiches.

BACK

Foundation row: With 9/I hook and MC, ch 53 loosely. Work 1 sc in third ch from hook, * 1 dc in next ch, 1 sc in next ch, rep from * end 1 sc in last ch, ch 3, turn (counts as a dc).

Row 1: * Work 1 sc in next dc, 1 dc in next sc, rep from * across, ending 1 sc in top of tch. Ch 3 (counts as dc), turn.

Rep row 1 for patt. Work patt for 11½" (29.3 cm), fasten off.

FRONT

Work same as back.

GUSSET

With 9/I hook and MC, ch 13. Work patt for 38" (96.5 cm), fasten off.

LARGE POCKETS

Make two.
With 9/I hook and MC, ch 53. Work patt for 6" (15 cm), fasten off.

SIDE POCKETS

Make two.
With 9/I hook and MC, ch 13. Work patt for 6½" (16.3 cm), fasten off.

With 9/I hook and CC, ch 7. Work patt for 45" (115 cm), fasten off.

BUTTON TAB

With 9/I hook and MC, ch 13. Work patt for 3½" (9 cm).

Next row: Work patt for 3 sts, ch 4, sk 4, work patt for last 3 sts, ch 1, turn.

Next row: Work 1 sc in each of first 3 sts, 4 sc under ch-4 lp, sc in last 3 sts, fasten off.

FINISHING

1. Usi   d CC, work 1 row sc at the top edge of all the pockets.

2. Sew t.   k pockets in place.

3. Fold the   in at the center bottom, pin the sides in place. Working from.   ing at the top edge, with 8/H hook and CC, work-ing through boi.   n down one side, along the bottom, up the other side. Work the ot.   espond.

4. Sew the side pockets   place on the gusset.

5. Sew the straps in place, sewing through the pocket and bag to form divisions in the large pocket.

6. Using MC and 8/H hook, work 1 row sc around the entire top of the bag.

7. Sew the tab in place. Sew on the button.

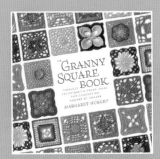

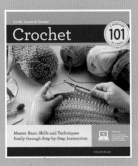

For more technique instructions and projects look for these books.

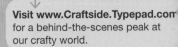

The Granny Square Book

978-158923-638-7

The Complete Photo Guide to Crochet

978-158923-472-7

Crochet 101

978-158923-639-4

This material originally appeared in the books *Hooked Bags* (ISBN: 978-1-58923-255-6), *Hooked Throws* (ISBN: 978-1-58923-267-9), *Hooked Hats* (ISBN: 978-1-58923-256-3), *The Granny Square Book* (978-1-58923-638-7), and *Knit or Crochet–Have It Your Way* (978-1-58923-431-4) by Margaret Hubert.

Visit www.Craftside.Typepad.com for a behind-the-scenes peak at our crafty world.

Printed in China
ISBN: 978-1-58923-771-1

YRNBK

$12.99 US / £7.99 UK / $14.99 CAN

0 52944 01942 6

9 781589 237711   51299